# Emily and Other Poems

by

**Gordon Greenall**

To Helen
Kindest regards
Gordon Greenall

**GEMINI**

Also published by Gemini:
The poorest he by Victoria Bennett

**Published in Great Britain 2005 by Gemini**
High Street, Chipping Campden, Glos, GL55 6AG



ISBN 0 – 9547600-1-8

Printed by Vale Press Ltd
6 Willersey Business Park, Willersey,
Worcestershire, WR12 7RR
Tel: 01386 858900

# Contents

# Introduction

Gordon Greenall was born in the small Cotswold market town of Chipping Campden in 1945. His father, George, worked as a builder and farm labourer. In retirement, he took it upon himself to act as guide to the many tourists who visited the town. Gordon's mother, the eponymous Emily, was from Herefordshire. Orphaned at the age of ten, at twelve she went into service and later worked as a chambermaid in Cheltenham and finally in a hotel in Chipping Campden where she met and married George. At eleven, Gordon went to the town's ancient Grammar School but left without academic qualifications.

Gordon is an observer. As a boy walking home from school he remembers watching the hungry, dusty men working on The Thrashing Drum. This poems recalls a vanished world but not necessarily a world mourned by the poet; "Work began with instant dust/ From the dried and empty husk" or in The Ploughman, "Years break down the ground/ Wear out the man and horse", and in "Lambing" the shepherd's "clock round shift has took a toll" .

Gordon's poems reveal much about his own life. In The Ferret, the reader senses his boyish pride at being taken rabbiting by his father when he writes of the ferret, "Then he travels along by bike/In a bag upon my back". There is an understandable bitterness in Creation, a poem about his schooling. He writes of his teachers, "They made me feel down/ Mixing the grease paint to put on my face/ Creating the mask of a clown." When Gordon left school at the age of sixteen, he was taken on as a builder's labourer. His powers of description and attention to detail, which lend an immediacy to his poems, are evident in The Stone Dressing. The pieces of stone are "like walnut fists" the "ruddy wrists" of the "bankers" are "copper banded". The labourers dressed the stone when the weather prevented other work and they "rain the axes down/ ....Without respite from cold and pain". Gordon was glad when he became apprenticed to a carpenter and was no longer required to do this arduous work.

Many of Gordon's interests are solitary; exploring the hedgerows and walking in the hills, and his concern for nature and animal instincts are the subject of so many of his poems. In The Falcon's Sky, he captures the patience of the bird of prey, "Wide balanced wings are spread/ To hold his watching perch." While his poem, The Hawthorn Tree, reveals Gordon's love of his native Cotswold landscape, "Growing from a limestone base.....A solid resistant wall she stands....With tiny buds of vivid green". In Nesting Sparrows the reader shares the poet's wonderment at the birds' determination to survive and reproduce, "scraps of carrion/ Won in battle raged with finches" . In Broken Water Music, the scene is so vividly set, "And see the thrashing water fight/ Turn from babbling argument to a rapid tumbling war", that the reader is with the poet watching as the fisherman's "rod is cast to catch the dancing reeled carp and flight/ Of a courting bream." Gordon has a countryman's respect for weather and seasons. In White Roads, the snow causes "self-inflicted long delay/ Upon the homeward ice-bound chill highway", and in Falling Leaves, "..we are only ever bystanders/ Without influence or power to change" .

A holiday in the Highlands of Scotland inspired "South Flows the Burn" and the memorable opening line, "From birthing, craggy darkness", while Plantation House and Melting Ice and Liquid Snow are the result of a visit to America.

Aged fifty-five, Gordon had to retire from his work as a fireman which he had been for twenty-one years. Retirement gave Gordon time to reflect and his poems are a result of these thoughts. He writes powerfully about fire in Raging

Night. The title refers not just to the energy of fire - the flames are “Pulled from sleep to dance” - but to the anger felt by firemen who risk their lives because of others’ negligence, “ find the careless culprits/ And to them apportion blame.” As a fire-fighter, Gordon was often at the scene of road accidents and Heroines is a tribute to paramedics. In later years he took part, as a fireman, in the local Remembrance Day parades and he has written several war poems. His grandfather ran away from Campden as a sixteen-year-old lad and joined a Liverpool Regiment and later the Royal Gloucesters. As a professional soldier, he served in the Boer War and the First World War. Gordon’s war poems dwell on the waste of life.

In May 2004 Gordon was diagnosed with leukaemia. His own illness has lead to a preoccupation with death both his own, as in The Grisly Queue, and that of others, as in his two poems about a friend’s wife, Rachel.

Anger is not far from the surface in much that Gordon writes. One concern is the way that wishes of ordinary people are ignored by politicians, as in Dying Youth and Seniors’ Service. He also rails against institutions’ insensitivity to the needs of the individual, as in Creation. In Reality, the anger turns to joy, “But I am the man I want to be/ Not the man they made of me.” While The Waiting Room displays resignation, Cold is the Dusk and Yuletide Yesterday deal with the poet’s hatred of injustice and man’s indifference to suffering. The cruelty of unrequited love is also touched on in Beach Girl and Dark Desire, among others.

In contrast to the above concerns, Gordon has written a number of humorous verses featuring the antics of local characters, now gone, whom he so admired in his youth. These poems contain a certain amount of Cotswold dialect to give a flavour of the local language. As in oral tradition, they are tales that Gordon recalls having been told or stories that, given the natures of the characters, are likely to have happened. In this selection of poems there is room for just a few, namely, Amusin' Flimmy, Baldy's Bike, Cup's Dealin' and Rhubarb.

It is local conversation, the world about him, the sights, and sounds, and smells he has experienced, and the behaviour of people or animals observed in the world of country work and recreation, that have helped shape Gordon's voice. He does not read many other poets although he sometimes uses well tried forms for his poems. Both Broken Water Music and Grazing Cattle are in terza rima, The Grisly Queue and Melting Ice and Liquid Snow villanelles, while Flying Winter Clouds, Heroines, A Love of Trout, and Spring Music are sonnets.

In this selection the poems have been arranged alphabetically by title. The resulting order is, therefore, arbitrary, taking the reader on a journey of discovery, at one moment smiling with amusement at a character's deeds, the next breathless with the beauty of the scenery or full of wonder at the natural world, and finally reduced to tears because of the inevitable suffering of life and man's mortality.

V.B. March 2005

## Amusin' Flimmy

Ol' Flimmy was a walkin'
the road to the Battle Brook
when 'e started smilin'
at somethin' that 'is fancy took.
Perhaps it was the pipe
'e'd filled with ol' black shag,
or maybe it was them pheasants
'e was a carryin' in 'is bag.

Or maybe the weather was pleasin'
as it was sunny, warm, an' fine
but perhaps it was the fact
we was now on summer time.
Or the wild flowers' pastel shades
paintin' the fields of growin' 'ay.
Or it could have bin 'twas Friday
startin' Whitsun 'oliday.

As I stepped from Stanley's Orchard
I was still a wonderin' why
when I noticed the apple blossom
that could have caught 'is eye.
Then we met upon the road
for 'is was an easy pace
an' I couldn't 'elp but notice
the smile broad across 'is face.

Just then a young lad came up.
Ol' Flimmy called 'im "Ron."
I never saw a longer face
on such a youthful mon.
'e said 'is wife 'ad left 'im.
All 'is savings they was gone.
An' 'is next door neighbour's wife
was two weeks late a-comin' on.

Flimmy told me that 'er 'usband
'ad bin a year away
an' now 'e is expected
back 'ome 'ere any day.
Then Flimmy says, "I 'as t' smile
when I sees 'ow trouble comes.
Young Ron, 'e should know better
than t' pick 'is neighbour's plums."

## Autumn Fall

The green leaves of summer
Turn fire-red and gold,
Yellow, brown and rusty
As they begin to grow old.
A sight of nature's wonder
Displayed without a sound
As silently they fall
In a cascade to the ground.
Blown like elfish dancers,
Racing around naked trees.
Their tireless cavorting lasts
Until the ebb of the last breeze
Drops them now slow decaying,
Cocoa dark and coffee lees,
Feeding new spring growth
Waited on by wild bumble bees.

## Autumn Travel

Autumn's swirling dampness belies
The signs of frost upon my head.
Ridge and furrow fields reflected
In an ever more sagging, bagging face,
Showing the years of journeys to the sea
Battered by frothy breakers on a craggy shore,
Hiding signs of wear and tear
Like shaving foam upon my jaw.

My part in this pageant has overrun.
A role I sought never to play. Even a day
Is far too long, each hour darkened by
The shadow of its superseding hour.
Travel is in my nature now, satisfying
A great desire to reach my goals,
To stride apace into every space
That lies between the freezing poles.

To see battlefields, and oil well yields,
Smoking stacks, and back to backs,
From tops of mountains and water fountains.
Nothing wasted - all smelled and tasted,
Strolling in pastures of flattish green.
Or, on sailing ship, I take the helm
To float across, an even flatter sea
Before time takes me to another realm.

A realm of reckless flings and fallen kings
While beggars, late at the Pearly Gate,
Hide low guile behind each sallow smile
As they conspire to cheat the Devil's fire.
Where the silence of the owl
Drowns the chilling howl
From the east wind's gusty blow
Of twenty or so degrees below.

Now my journey, fraught with thought
Of complete rejection, upon inspection,
Has entered the gate to the final straight,
To defend the sagging spirit to the end.
The judgement, weighed and made,
Is pronounced to one and all.
There are no smiles nor tears from me
As I am led to Valhalla's concert hall.

## Baldy's Bike

Ol' Baldy's bike 'ad broke
with a puncture in the tyre
that 'appened quite soon a'ter
'e'd rode over some barbed wire.
Now, if 'e did stop t' walk
then 'e surely would be late.
So, 'e rode upon the 'andlebars
t'even out 'is 'eavy weight.

All went well at first
as 'e rode along the straight
but just around the corner
was where 'e 'ad a change of fate.
The slope started off down 'ill
for just the first short part,
then Baldy went around the bend
into a 'orse drawn rubbish cart.

A lot of noise was 'eard
as Baldy flew through the mornin' air
'ead-first into the scrappy's load
landin' in an ol' bath chair.
'e realised that all 'e'd 'urt
was a big slice of 'is pride
but more trouble was a-comin'
on 'is runaway dust cart ride.

Resultin' from the accident
the driver 'ad been thrown off
an' was unable to remount,
bein' not quite quick enough.
This meant Baldy was alone,
with a runaway ton of trash,
as the 'orse went through the crossin'
causin' the up 'ill train t' crash.

The Station Master was aghast
an' flew into a rage.
'e grabbed Ol' Baldy by the coat
an' locked 'im in the bullock cage.
A police inspector then arrived
t' sort out the awful mess.
'e gave instructions for t' clear the place
an' put Baldy in duress.

The magistrate fined Baldy
an' said, "I've never seen the like,
of so much damage done
by a bald man with a bike."
He then looked straight at Baldy
sayin', "Seven days or pay your due.
And when your bike's repaired
Be sure both tyres are brand new."

Baldy's pockets, they was bare
so, 'e would 'ave 'ad t' do the time
until the prosecutor said,
"I've something better on my mind."
The inspector told Ol' Baldy,
"I will spare you bars and warder
If you're prepared to accept the terms
of a Special Service Order."

'e 'ad t' mend the pot'oles
in five miles of major roads,
an' clean out a dozen ponds
for spawning frogs and toads.
Finally the clerk read out,
t' the sound of Baldy's moans,
the order also made requirement of
'im losing several stones.

Baldy's life was changed for ever
with 'is eatin' cut in 'alf,
an' all that 'eavy labourin'
left 'im wi'out the strength t' laugh.
But 'is downfall was the frogs
what caused a gret big riot
for 'e'd used their long 'ind legs
t' supplement 'is meagre diet.

## Beach Girl

Kicking at the surf
In a swollen blue sea,
Looking back at the
Young lady looking at me.
Bikini clad perfection
Brightening the beach,
But, like the sunset,
She's just out of reach.

Her hair is long
And delightfully flowing.
Her cheeks are pink
And gently glowing.
Her distant blue eyes
Leave a hint on her face
That her mind is not here
But in some faraway place.

We look at each other
But our eyes never meet.
She looks at my hands.
I look at her feet.
I'm totally enchanted
By all that I see
But I haven't a notion
What she thinks of me.

The theme of my dreams
Is shaped like the dunes
Blown by the winds
Around Jupiter's moons.
She dapples the sands
With long golden hair
Then dives with the sunset
Somewhere out there.

My feet start to walk.
They are carrying me
Through the fine shingle
To the swollen blue sea.
The waves take my breath
As I'm washed from the beach.
My thoughts stay with her
But she's far out of reach.

## Black Bin Bag

How fortunate the bin men came
To take those bags stood in the rain,
Stacked, and waiting overnight
For transport to the landfill site.
Rubbish tossed within a sack
Into the waiting dustcart back.
Tons of dumpage crushed in haste
Compacting toxic household waste.

What treasure has been cast within
The badly dented rubbish bin?
A 'five-pence-off' detergent box,
Three multicoloured woollen socks,
A Christmas assortment biscuit tin,
The broken neck of a violin,
A mouldy, greenish hot cross bun,
And a badly split black wellington,

Strawberry yoghurts out of 'sell-by',
Rotten tomatoes bought to fry.
A burned and blackened frying pan,
Someone's breakfast baked bean can,
A stale loaf, half chewed by mice,
A take-away tray of prawn fried rice,
An old, moth eaten silk top hat,
And jars filled up with cooking fat,

Grandma's hatbox with a dent,
A broken bottle, once filled with scent,
Empty beer cans drunk at home,
A bottle drained of Cotes du Rhone,
Overalls with sewn on patches,
Programmes from past football matches,
Waxed milk cartons with a smell
And old chicken bones as well.

Remember the days of soft, fish paste-
Times when there wasn't ever waste?
The boiled scraps and potato peel
Fed to chickens for their meal.
Cut-down clothes, and cobbled shoes
And nothing in the shops to choose.
People dressed in pre-war fashions
And, worst of all, those awful rations.

To those who vent nostalgic sighs
For rummage sales and 'bring and buys',
Being heard and never seen
And standing up for her, the Queen,
I feel that I am bound to say,
"You can keep each bygone day."
They are welcome to the Empire flag;
I'd rather have my black bin bag.

## Blossoming

Hail the coming early light of May
Christening with buds
Each tree
Set with nectar's petal rings,
Drawing wild bees
To pollinate a later fruit display.

Innocent stands the cherry
In her blossom dress,
Fresh frocked
As if to wed the coming spring,
Then swell in truth
To fruit with ripened berry.

While patiently waits the pear,
In her awkwardness,
To catch
The tossed bouquet of spring,
And form a club
For all hopefuls gathered there.

Most heavy bears the plum,
In blooming splendour
Full weight,
To meet the 'Harvest Home'
Of those already here
And those yet to come.

Over all displays the rich damson,
Shedding her spring coat
To show
Those densest purple orbs
Of deeper taste
To claim the prize is won.

But beware the darkly spreading brier
Clad in ragged dress.
Her fruits lurk
To lure, with taste and form
From within a suit of thorny cloth,
And scratch a man's desire.

## Broken Water Music

Those large rocks, spread wide across the stream,
Break up the water's flow
And disturb the silence of my dream.

They babble as in argument – as if in need to know.
Can they ever lie at rest
Or must they forever onwards go?

For water's whole environment lives best
In active bustle
Away from green stagnation that will become a turgid pest.

Movement brings strength to her muscle
At a freshening speed
Which adds a greater power to her tenants' cleansing tussle.

And manna, brought as maggot, high carrion, and dry seed,
Washes through this shaded place
For the quick and watching to reach, to take, then feed.

As the late budding ash filters light to halve with grace,
And spread it on the forest floor
As though with a cloth of fine and darkened patchwork lace.

I'm drawn from those curtailed dreams to raise my head once more
And see the thrashing water fight
Turn from babbling argument to rapid tumbling war.

My rod is cast to catch the dancing reeled carp and flight
Of courting bream
Before my water hunting is expunged by the mantle of the night.

Leaving those large rocks, spread wide across the stream,
To play the broken water
As music to return me slowly to the silence of my dream.

## Cold is the Dusk

Trudging under navy skies,
Over landscape of a winter's guise,
Lighted only by a pallid sun
Set low as early evening's done
The hills incline from dip to scarp
The frost increases from rhyme to sharp,
And leafless trees, in purple bark,
Stand – waiting for the coming dark.

Such a scene sets this length of way
For the many coated tramp a-sway,
Sallow skinned and unreplete,
From frosted nose to frozen feet.
His soles are worn and uppers holed
Unable now to stop the bitter cold
And laced to limbs that pain to bend
As slow they trudge to journey's end.

Each step rolls from heel to toe,
Echoing 'neath the roosting crow,
Tramping down the empty husk
Slower now in gathering dusk.
Hedgerows' long-shed, dying leaves
Blown by gusty, bitter thieves
Into piles, ripped and torn apart,
Like ever-changing modern art.

Full fallen is the freezing night,
Her blanket blacking all from sight.
Hidden now, stiff-fallen leaves
And their divested parent trees.
Impressive guards, they stand by day
But darkness conjures them away,
Replaced by those in nocturnal cause
Who seek their prey without a pause.

The night brings on constant change
With old dog fox, in vest of mange,
Mindful of the badger's swinging claw
While holding distance from his jaw.
Voles alert, through dead of night,
To the barn owl's noiseless flight.
And insects scavenge every kind
Of scattered debris left behind.

Good conscience should not allow
A 'down and out' left to the bough
But morning light shows up the ward
To find the traveller still abroad,
Abandoned to a fearful fate
Stiff and lifeless, close to churchyard gate.
For want of charity gone, unfound,
Within the sight of hallowed ground.

## Cold Work

Looking back I can recall
The coldest winter of them all.
Frost two foot in the ground,
Snow and ice sticking sound
To hill grass and meadow lea
And on a side of every tree,
Hedges stretching for fresh relief
From hard suffocation underneath.

Building sites were most affected
Being almost unprotected.
Soft stone took on a metal ping
Not unlike the church bell's ring.
Cave formations in piles of sand,
Tools frozen to the warmest hand,
And fires lit to ease and thaw
Were less effective more and more.

Some said the frost just couldn't hold
But the snow kept in the cold
Kept it in the stone and brick
Held it in every straw filled rick.
Joined timber joists and wooden rails
With frozen water screws and nails;
Welded clay against the plough
And froze the pigeon to the bough.

All manual work came to a halt
Except on roads in need of salt
To clear the snow turned ice
And rid the paths of winter's vice.
Men, up before the dawning day
To clear the travellers' weary way,
Suffering from the arctic blast,
Cursing each freezing day that passed.

Hands, chapped, and cold, and sore,
Bitten with chilblains by the score.
Nowhere for us to take a look
To see water flowing in the brook.
No grass on which the sheep could graze,
No end to those God-forsaken days,
No contented cattle lowing,
Just man's grumble, " It's still snowing".

The sun comes up so weak and pale
It hardly has the strength to sail
Across a darker even bleaker sky
But seems to find the need to try.
The farmer then gives us a shout
To see if we can help him out;
A ewe that was buried overnight
Comes out alive, to our delight.

Straw grass has bowed an empty head
Appearing as though it must be dead.
Petals still cling to wild rose,
Too cold to start to decompose.
The ash still holds a weight of seed
On which the birds have no will to feed.
Dormant is the flora flow
Suspended in the chilling snow.

Then one morning through the door
I witness signs of coming thaw.
Climate changes by degrees
Movements seen among the trees
Vegetation slowly comes to bud
Dormant mice awaken in the wood -
A frantic time to dash apace
To ensure the future of their race.

Many seasons have I lived through
Working at what I had to do,
With coat collar up around my face
Or stripped off down to my waist.
Some winters dry and bitter cold
Mild winters wet and growing mould,
But nothing like the one I do recall -
The coldest winter of them all.

## Copper Dreams

When I looked upon her face
I saw humour there,
With freckled decorations
Below a mop of bright red hair.
Navy-blue eyes with laughter lines
In a face of milk white skin
And bright red lips that pout
Above a dimpled, rounded chin.

She would stand displeased
With hand upon her hip,
And iceberg flashing teeth
Beneath a curling upper lip.
Perhaps I should speak to her
So that I may find
The smile that she has hidden
Inside her troubled mind.

I would like to let her know
I see her, as lit by astral light,
The brightest star way past Mars
That lights the heavenly night.
Perhaps I should have used
The spoken word instead
Of sending out, by silence,
The emotions boiling in my head.

There her smiling cheeks
Glow with pink perfection,
Laughing all around the room
Except in my direction.
Her hair of copper tints
Flows freely everywhere.
The part lit bronze is dancing
To the tune of my despair.

I know that it is best for me
To practise to forget
That fateful, windswept day
When rain and we first met.
But autumn's rusty colours,
And winter's fires, reflect
Sights that won't fade gracefully
Adding fuel to my regret.

## Creation

I was sent to school as a boy.
I went to school and they laughed.
The teachers were all in agreement –
They'd never taught one so daft.
I had difficulty seeing the blackboard.
I had difficulty seeing the words.
No chance of constructing a sentence –
I knew not my nouns from my verbs.

The teachers agreed I should leave
As soon as I possibly could,
Sure I could work in timber
For my head - it was made out of wood.
My first job was in the forest
On the end of a two-man saw.
The foreman said I was doing well
And in time would learn even more.

I saw millions of insects
And spiders with webs catching flies.
I watched long, furry caterpillars
Turn into red admiral surprise.
There were beetles and fleas,
There were wasps and wild bees,
There were seeds determined to grow
Into a forest of magnificent trees.

I wondered, " Who created this world?
Did He do it all on His own?"
It was certainly no one from my schooling,
None of the teachers I'd known.
They were too busy ridiculing,
Descending to humiliation,
While seeming so very confident
Of the success of my poor education.

They made me feel down -
Mixing the grease-paint to put on my face -
Creating the mask of a clown.
Trapping confusion with spite,
Ending the birth of healthy relations,
By shooting the dog that never would bite,
And leaving me floundering in the lurch,
Forcing me into the arms of the Church.

There was singing and chanting of prayers
That were said for the dead from the living.
I wasn't sure why I'd come over so cold
Perhaps it was the chill of misgiving.
Why, with the power to create the rain,
To fill the rivers, the lakes, and the pools,
Did God put all of our learning
In the hands of such arrogant fools?

## Cup's Dealin'

Last Sunday in the Bells was Cup
With a patch across 'is eye.
I was so concerned about 'is 'ealth
I went an' asked 'im, "Why?"
"Well," said Cup, "I bin a-sufferin' from
A clout an' some double-vision.
A glass uv whisky cured me yud
An' me vision's in remission."

Just then a mon came in
'e seemed a bumptious sort o' fella,
Shouted for a drink so loud
It brought ol' Jim up from the cellar.
" I'll have a 'gin and it'," sez 'e
Without so much as an invitation.
And then 'e sez, "My good man,
Arrange for me your taxi to the station."

Ol' Jim scowled an' sez, "It can't be done,
For I can't leave the bar,
An' there's no one else in 'ere
Can drive my motor car.
Ol' Cup steps in t' offer 'elp.
'e takes the key from off the shelf
An' tells the chap that, for a sum,
The car is 'is if 'e could drive 'isself.

The mon drank up an' turned t' Cup
An' gives 'im a carefully folded fiver.
Then, 'e leaves the pub a-mutterin',
"It's a lot for a car without a driver."
Well, you can imagine ol' Jim's reaction
When 'e sees 'is car 'as gone.
"You've bin an' lost me car," sez 'e,
"An' a fiver wun't buy me another one!"

"Don't panic, Jim," sez Cup,
"'e's on a nearly empty tank
With just enough in reserve
T' come back up station bank.
An' I also told the mon that
Sundays you charges double rate.
So, 'e'll be back 'specially when 'e finds
The last train left at 'alf-past eight."

Next day the mon returns
An' ol' Jim tells Cup t' sort it out.
Cup assures the mon, " I'm wrong;
O' that there is no doubt."
An' Cup returned 'is two pound ten
T' which the mon exclaimed, "I have been done."
Ol'Cup sez, " But this be Monday so
The refund be just a single one."

## Dark Desire

So prim and neat and dark
In high backed chair she sat
In satin lace trimmed frock
Beneath a wide brimmed hat.
Her hair shone, richly brown,
So dark it could be black,
In ebony turned ringlets
Hanging halfway down her back.

She, the centre of attraction
In the sunshine on the lawn,
Was holding court to all around
As she'd done since newly born.
Perfect forms, her jewel teeth
And blood filled lips
Formed a smile to stop my heart
And pulse my finger tips.

The Devil invited my eyes
To take her, soul and mind,
To explore her marble hall
And keep the jewels I find.
He whispers, " Lift her clothing
And touch the skin beneath;
Enjoy this body of pure delight
Carved in such a great relief."

My desire to be so near,
Of course, could never be.
Even if twinned with her desire
She wouldn't notice me.
For her face of sheer delight,
Lit with a welcome thought,
Extended only over those
Contained within her court.

Mixed were my emotions,
As I slowly turned away,
For I had not been cast a part
In her happy, birthday play.
To the gates in spirits low
I slipped, and nearly fell,
Lurching down the cinder path
Still caught in her dark spell.

## Disguise

Loneliness crept upon me
Dressed in shawl and cloak.
I did not recognise her
When at first She spoke,
Whispering softly to allay
The misgivings I did hear
And showed upon my furrowed brow
More deeply year by year.

"Come with me," She urged,
" To the valley of spring waters;
Cavort with me relentlessly
Make merry with my courtiers;
Step among the wild flowers,
Resplendent in the wood;
Throw off those cares you bear
In silence from your childhood.

Just mouth your every wish,
While drinking from my well,
And your life will turn about,
Commanded by my spell.
Give yourself up, as one
Who will take a wife and friend
To keep in his own company
Until he reaches "journey's end".

My joy was ill-considered.
I was cast in a shallow place,
Set to prevent life lived as
A child born so fair of face.
The power of darkness shook
The sunlight from my hair
And sent me on a journey
Dogged by more despair.

The partners of my dreams
Were those I could not trust.
They helped to build my castles
Which quickly turned to dust.
They set me on the road
Just as the darkness fell
And their laughter followed after me
On a journey into hell.

Distress loudly echoes
Around my short retirement,
But Loncliness still has her grip
And She will not relent.
I recognise the whispered words
From underneath her cowl.
The harshness of their message
Is broadened in her scowl.

Loneliness comes disguised
In sunlit yellow hair,
Piled wildly on perfection
To bring a long, lorn stare.
Or in a promise, sent
By the stretching hand held out,
Soon to be surrounded
By lies, deceit, and doubt.

She sometimes walks with me
And sometimes lies in wait.
On occasions, when I think She's gone,
She appears, arriving late.
My nightmares I must break
Or slip beneath the wire
Where I am bound to burn
Alone in everlasting fire.

## Dust

Dust crushed and sifted
From particles and grains
To lay as mineral - organic -
Or degraded human dead remains.
Each surrenders colour
To a formal black or charcoal grey
But who can tell the difference
On a cold November day?

Dust blown around the room
Or lying deathly still
Upon the grand piano,
Bookshelf, or window sill.
Each particle takes a grain of shine away
Put on with elbow-grease and polish spray.
But who will see the loss
On a dull November day?

Dust falls upon the streets
To be churned by walking heels,
The fog-bound choking breeze
And the turning traffic wheels.
Each, as much as any other,
Becomes a part of urbanised decay.
But who will even notice
On a dank November day?

Dust forms up with veterans
Who march to their own Cenotaph
Displaying dead men's medals
Proudly worn on their behalf.
Each grain stings a leathered face
Returned from Ypres or Souvla Bay.
But who will soon remember
On a drear November day?

Dust fills their throats
And cuts into their eyes;
Chokes these sentinel old men
With their faltering last goodbyes,
Each grain more cutting than before
As this final time they pray.
So who will hear again
The silence of this November day?

## Dying Youth

Under Beeching's axe my station fell.
Her Great Western Pride
Pushed aside
By bulldozer blade,
Sending her broken parts
To boost a dead museum trade.
While a comprehensive bill
Was born to kill
My old school as well.

Local hospitals caused to fall,
On their own land
By blackened hand,
Taking away the surgeon's knife.
To be replaced with private enterprise –
A profit driven life.
While the live-stock market, now
Will not, somehow,
Be reopened after all.

Powerful elms once stood erect
Until, in the dark,
Death - beetle under bark -
Reduced English lanes,
Of growing highs and lows,
To flat remains.
While ditches are buried under fill,
Against good Nature's will,
And those people who object.

The melody of rural concert gone -
Infested by din,
Brought in
By megawatted power,
Drowning the sweetest song
Of finches' music hour.
While insecticides dispatch
The flying catch
Of food they used to lived on.

Secret Whitehall mandarins apply
Their legislation,
To our irritation,
Of registration cards
And CCTV. And help metrication
Kill our stones and yards
While new inventions
Complicate our pensions.
Perhaps to urge we old to die?

# Emily

## *Going back*

The noisy, bustling station
Seemed to fade into retreat
As she entered her compartment
And sank into her seat.
Her many mixed emotions
Were kept hidden well inside
For she was much a lady
With no outward show of pride.

A window was slightly open
To let in the smell of smoke
While the solid bogie-wheels
With the iron rails spoke.
Their sound was punctuated
By the chattering rail joints
And the rhythmic passing over
Of endless, well worn points.

As the journey quickened,
Through the urban sprawl
Into the evening countryside,
Came sights she could recall.
Memories came flooding back
Of those times before the war
When men and women danced
To music played no more.

The warmth of those memories
Seemed to wrap around her
As did her woollen coat,
With protection, as it bound her.
The best of Harris Tweed
Woven in a Hebridean land
Kept warm the distant memories
As would a glove a frosted hand.

She could see clear pictures
From her long and hard won past,
Recalling wartime blackout
And damage from bomb blast,
'Make do and mend' old dresses,
Work as a nursing volunteer,
The emptiness from lack of food
And the stomach churning fear.

The past, she felt, was best
Abandoned to the ancient bones
Fleshless now, in ghoulish mask,
Marked by crumbling marker stones.
Wilting blooms long carried off,
As she was destined to become,
Were lost in death's cold silence
And single beating drum.

## *Awake*

Emily full-dressed had lain
Throughout a sleepless night
In the attic room she shared
With her sister, infant mite.
Their single iron bedsteads sat
Side by side behind the door,
With only painted chest of drawers
Besides, upon the boarded floor.

She was filled with silent tears,
Pained and short of breath,
Unable yet to take in the news
Of her mother's awful death.
The mantel clock chimed five
To Emily, herself a month past ten,
And her sister, lost in fitful sleep,
Both never to see their mother again.

An early breeze blew in
To bring the start of day,
Producing sun-shaft pastel shades
Through the early morning grey.
Emily closed her weeping eyes
To weave a hat with sunshine straw.
Then tied a bow of pink dawn rays
To make the hat her mother wore.

A maiden aunt, brought in,
Called up the winding stairs.
Her shrill shout, "Up! Get up!"
Caught Emily unawares.
As she wiped away the tears
Her hands seemed cast in lead,
In prayer, asking to remain
Secure, tucked up in bed.

## *Parted*

Friday came in fitful grey
Bringing spots of drizzling rain.
How sad they looked to Emily,
As they died against the window pane,
Reflecting how she felt
Cold and much distressed.
For today her mother would be laid
Down to her final rest.

She thought of last July
And the picnic that they took,
Wrapped in little paper parcels
Placed in a basket with a book.
Emily could hear their laughter,
Competing with a choir of birds.
So much joy and merriment:
On a day of no unhappy words.

She vowed to hold these memories
Inside her broken heart for
Those impossible black moments
Of her mother's sad departure.
She would not look upon the day
Through tear stained eyes of grief
But think of paper parcels
Filled with joy and gay relief.

During the grim proceedings
She would close, for a while,
Her welling, clear grey eyes
And see her mother's smile.
As the droning dirge was fading
She heard her mother gently say,
"You will have more paper parcels
as we did that picnic day."

## *Her Realm*

Tender were the words that spilled
From her mother's lips
As she made her way to pick
September haws and hips.
In the sultry summer haze
Of morning's sky blue suit
With just a hint of freshness
She gathered early morning fruit.

A thrush flew from an elder bush,
With fledglings she was bound -
On the move, with cheery song,
To a fresher hunting ground.
Here the cruelty of the world
Was banished far away,
Among the new mown barley fields
Where half grown rabbits played.

Emily twirled around in circles,
Her basket reaching out,
To the members of her family
Her mind had brought about.
They were dressed in Sunday best,
Their faces, smiling, open wide.
Such company and laughter
Filled Emily with a lasting pride.

They would take, together
With Emily's slender hands,
The rose hips from the shrubs
Growing wild within those lands.
The lunch, it would be taken
On the church clock's single chime
And Emily would return
To her 'other summer time.'

## *Alone*

The dogcart rattled to a halt
Close to the picket gate.
Even ill-lit night could not
Make the old conveyance late.
The driver, muffled against
The chill of autumn's early bite,
Tottered on war bent legs
Now far too old to fight.

Painfully he raised her bag
And, limping, carried out
All her worldly goods
Wrapped up in lonely doubt.
Tears welled in her eyes,
Her throat was set to choke.
As she, in hurting silence, left
No one remaining spoke.

A frail waif stood Emily
On the verge of desperation.
At the end of childhood
Drowned in adult expectation.
Toys, no more to dress,
For games no longer played,
Put away for ever. Now replaced
By the job of serving maid.

Her mind and body fell
Into a world of dirty grates:
Hands starched whitened laundry
And polished silver plates.
And cold, flagstone steps
Were scrubbed on knees to meet
The demand of trodden grime
From rich, well-heeled feet.

Ground from sleep to dark
By endless chores and chivvying
A young girl's dreams were choked
In gasps of breathless skivvying.
Each month she was allowed
To rest for half a day,
Reminded that she must post home
Her hard earned meagre pay.

## *Full Grown*

Emily is now full grown,
Tall and straight of back,
Filled with practised arts
That many others lack.
She uses hard won rights
Gained in growing up alone
Proudly showing suffragettes
Emancipation of her own.

Well dressed in fashions
From designers of the day,
Poised in perfect make-up
Hearing quiet whispers say,
" Who is she? - So statuesque,
Porcelain face on slender frame,
Wrapped in silk and calf skin."
More in mystery than from fame.

Her time is here and now –
To last a youthful spring,
A time to enjoy the feeling
That those admiring glances bring,
Sending blood to sensitise
The enrichment of desire,
Rising above her hesitation
To feel the heat of passion's fire.

Her fields, full of memories,
Are gone into a patchwork fold
As maturity has set her down
In streets said 'paved with gold',
Where there are no mother's whispers
Nor the parcels she was shown,
For Emily must make her way
In a life where she is cast alone.

## Empty Attic

Bright, sunlit patches,
Almost harsh,
Mark their path upon the winding stairs
Pitched with such a climb
They catch one unawares.

The tight landing's way is barred,
Caged
By the loft door louvres spilling light,
To lie side by side with shadow
Like a monochrome mosaic upon the winding flight.

The old door stiffly creaks, then slowly opens wide
To show inside
A thicket of uncoppiced spiders' silken lairs,
Covered in a growth of dust
Thickening each slender strand of cobweb hairs.

Motionless, the swell of dark-cast spiders wait
With sticky bait,
Bloated by decaying corps of flies,
Held in suspense by moisture drops
To stare out like drowning, disembodied eyes.

A lining hangs in drawn cream shreds,
As silk innards
From a velvet coat - once of ripest hawthorn red -
Now aged, to a dulled-down, purple plum,
Lying, stained and torn, as rags upon the unmade bed.

A mix of oils, crystallised and petrified to dust,
Coat a spangled palette
With summer green, a weeping blue, and brown.
While long-stiffened hair and bristle brushes
Remain, dropped upside down in a water jar to drown.

On the easel a canvas, waiting to be spread with utmost care,
Is empty yet.
His random woodcut picture blocks
Lie scattered over time with
Her opened pattern books of spring and summer frocks.

Though the trodden boards give out their creaking woes
They will not disclose
Who showed his art in wooden picture blocks
Nor who laid his thoughts in seas of oils' heavy hues
Nor even who was she who cut and stitched those summer frocks.

## Face to Face

A cold presence is,
I feel, within these churchyard walls,
Watching in chill silence
Beneath the reaching spire.
My stillness, of all but living breath,
Is brought about by deep emotion
In this yard of death
Where men with spirits do conspire.

I must soon move
Across this cold, unforgiving ground
To my cousin's grave
Dug in circumstances so distressing.
I kneel to say a late goodbye,
In croaking voice,
As I feel an urge to beg
For his forgiveness – if not his blessing.

I am scrawny,
Hair and bone like a sickly lurcher dog.
The tumour deep inside
Now has the best of me.
It grows and swells,
As a bitter pill,
Inside my shrinking bowels,
On course to take the rest of me.

Pomp and ceremony were done
By those who mourned
Before they left you, their son,
Committed to this awful midnight place,
Said to be forever lit
By God's good grace.
Then, too full of guilt, as you know,
I could not come.

Now, for forty years,
You have been laid at your long rest.
It was my finger that squeezed
To fire that fatal blast.
Thus here am I knelt
With heavy heart,
My remorse so keenly felt,
So ill-prepared to face you in the past.

## The Falcon's Sky

To hunt above the earth
The searching falcon flies
To swoop upon his prey
From his station in the skies,
His livery of dark grey splash
With black is keenly flecked
As he dives to take the flight
Of a lark with due respect.

Wide balanced wings are spread
To hold his watching perch
From where he spots a shape
To reward his silent search.
As he interrupts the vole
(At his seven second meal)
With such a driving force
He chokes its final squeal.

Sweeping eyes pick out
The dancing, brindle buck
Whose life is now, in seconds,
By the diving raider took
Away to the top of hollow oak
Where nestling young await
To strip and swallow flesh
Down their giant hunger-gape.

His hunting takes him over
A fresh thatched barley rick.
Till observation leads him
To spot an errant peewit chick
Whose early running spree
Will not give him time to grow -
In a flash its youth harsh drowned
In the falcon's fierce flow.

The warming April skies
Give up the tranquil peace
As Nimrod plummets through
A migrant skein of geese.
Oh! to be as he,
To float over the marbled trees,
And stand above the game
To take as one would please.

## Falling Leaves

The wind creates the form
Of her liquid sculptures
By blowing autumn leaves
Without firm intention
To either cause offence
Or yet to please.
And whispers her true gratitude,
For the freshness of those burnished sheddings,
To the dormant winter trees.

Then how wind's wrath can show,
As a heaving gale force,
To rip apart the lay,
Bringing change to rearrange
Leaves' line along the route
Of cold Remembrance Day.
Now once green chestnut hands
Are strewn upon the ground
In shuffling dull decay.

Though now, through bare branches,
We see high-steepled mountains climb
As if to journey far above the greying sky,
Their shadows fall over all.
While virgin snowcaps drop and rise
Like giant seagulls, on the fly,
Set in black, quiet mockery
Of the coming night.
Silent. As bats would be, when passing by.

Held is this scene by a moment's eye
Until everdarkening seconds
Bring the black night's curtain fall
To deny us such an impressive sight.
Further time hangs,
Like a stunning backdrop, to this autumn ball.
Leaves cavorting all the more,
Their skirmishes still heard aloud
But by sight lost to all.

By day we may watch in wonder
Or we may, simply, turn our backs
Upon this whirling weather architect.
But we are only ever bystanders
Without influence or power to change,
Or even stop and redirect,
This awesome exhibition
Of gale-swept sculptures brushed in delight
Or of orphans blown by ill neglect?

## The Ferret

The ferret has pink eyes
And cream and yellow hair.
He is such a quiet chap
You'd hardly know he's there.
Some people say he smells
But I've never known him rude.
He's one of my very best friends
And helps to catch my food.

He lives in a wooden cage
Until he's put into a sack.
Then he travels along by bike
In a bag upon my back.
Here he settles down to sleep,
Well, after all, it's dark,
Until awakened by the sniffing
And Jack Russell's mouthy bark.

He doesn't need much training
To know what he's about.
He descends into the burrow
To drive the rabbits out.
There's silence for a while
Followed by a muffled sound
Like a low, dull rumbling
That comes from underground.

A crash. A rush.
And then the rabbits fly.
The quickness of their flight
Almost beats the human eye,
Then the crafty poacher,
With reactions just as quick,
Has those dashing fur balls
Hocked and on the stick.

The ferret then returns
To a day so sharp and bright
He has to blink his eyes
To adjust them to the light.
Then he's back in his sack
And travelling home with me.
Forget the bread 'n' dripping
We'll be having rabbit pie for tea.

## Flying Winter Clouds

A skein of greylag geese will fly
In airborne, geometric, delta form
From their tundra grass to winter by
The stream, made oxbow with their swarm,
As a large, bedraggled gaggle set webbed feet
Upon the soft, close-padded, mossy stand,
To stake a claim on this fair country seat
And call this realm a make-do arctic land.

Now, all you scurrying tufted ducks,
Sent into noisome exile like a flapping train,
Must settle to the mud of cress-filled brooks
'til Spring brings back your mating field again.
So, give not this arctic interruption your best
For the wet lands will be returned in time for you to nest.

## Fresh Reflections

Dormant lies the headland field
In her quiet majesty,
With loam and stony overcoat,
Left to a fallow rest.
Her face looks in silence
From unblemished cope,
Without the grazing sheep or cow
Nor scarred by hoof and plough.

The absence of those formal rows,
Sown as man's drilled crops,
Are slow replaced by wild seeds
Inviting me, in boyish joy,
To amble waywardly
Across a natural greensward
Of grasses, couch, and margin sedge
Reaching out to briar hedge.

Nature serenades me
With a rare seduction of her sounds,
As a quartet of lowly willows
Back the screeching owl
In a disparate burst
To herald in the dusk,
And drown the vixen's bark
So sharp it could pierce the blackest dark.

Now, rid of all gathered doubt,
My empty mind takes up
The lilt of a westering tune
Blown, on the reeds of my mind,
With the flats and sharps
Of Irish harps
Coming clear from Kildare,
Wexford, or the County of Clare.

My mortality stands
While my mind speeds far,
Spinning with swarming fireflies
That flicker like marmalade sparks
To reel around my head,
Letting a wealth of new contradictions
Form as grains, in conception,
To be cast in a field of fresh reflections.

## Grazing Cattle

There were cattle in the field next door.
Some, with calves, stood grazing.
I'd never seen these beasts kept in there before.

A bull is close, his hackles raising,
Clawing at the dusty ground,
Head thrown high and nostrils blazing.

From the lane there comes a barking sound.
A farm dog has broken out -
Either collie bitch or mongrel hound.

The cowman, with his big toe gout,
Limps lamely to the gate
To find out what the fuss is all about.

He turns, and hops at quickened rate,
Knowing that he may be caught
Starting on the second milking hours late.

Perhaps he thinks he ought
To call for more help from his wife,
But he knows that her favours can't be bought.

So, alone, he faces the lonely, calloused strife
Of milking till it is all done,
As done as he will be when passing from this life.

## The Grisly Queue

The fresh dug grave, that waits in grisly open view,
Swallows the sombre, wrapped, and boxed remains.
So, tell me, who stands next at the head of the dead man's queue?

Comfort is too scarce for those sad, gathered few,
Called to stand in the headstone field and look upon
The fresh dug grave that waits in grisly open view.

The sexton comes, with spade and shovel crew,
To rain a soil cover down upon the shrouded bones.
So, tell me, who stands next at the head of the dead man's queue?

Wreaths, lain wet with tears now sated by the dew,
Slowly brown and wither as they lie adjacent to
The fresh dug grave that waits in grisly open view.

An old ewe watched as the black cock raven flew
Across the soon forgot washed and whitened bones.
So, tell me, who stands next at the head of the dead man's queue?

The hand of chance scythes down, at random, through
Life and takes the gross remains to partly fill
The fresh dug grave that waits in grisly open view.
So, tell me, who stands next at the head of dead man's queue?

## The Hawthorn Tree

The place that I most like to be
Is in the land of the hawthorn tree.
Growing from a limestone base
Into the air her branches chase,
Dark and twisted, in a winter's sky,
A lack of leaves but protected by
An intricate web of thorny spikes
Keeping guard as lancers' pikes.

The hawthorn in a field may stand
Looking out over grazing land.
Or planted, in ribbed line, to grow
Into a boundary's high hedgerow,
Guarding against the straying stock,
Protecting the newly planted crop.
A solid, resistant wall she stands
As protector of these cropping lands.

Punctuating the changing scene,
With tiny buds of vivid green,
She's first to signal coming spring,
Cueing wintering birds to sing,
Providing them with a place to rest
Scavenged scraps that form their nest,
And helping with their frantic search
To find a springtime courting perch.

To the hawthorn, sheep may guide
Their lambs to feed on the leeward side.
And, sheltering from the eastern blow,
Dress her up in drifts of woolly snow.
Rabbits dash to her safe embrace
For protection from the hunting race
Of dogs disgorged from the backs of cars
To chase hapless mammals in unequal wars.

Her buds are bursting now with green intent
But, for a month to June, they must relent
To blossom, filling the hedge with flowers –
Building salmon-pink and snow-white towers,
For there is no other tree or sedge
That could hope to decorate an English hedge
With such reach and walk of wild display
As that put on by blossom of the May.

## Heroines

The red sports car and the large yellow van,
Like quick robin and jaundiced mountain man,
Meet head-on, as Arthur's knights once would,
In twisting armour shells, slowly letting English blood.
Their near death embrace is over in a flash,
Not seen by those, who only heard the grinding crash,
Obliged now to stop in their own less pressing strife
To take on those grizzly tasks that might just save a life.

But then sirens, horns, and lights of flashing blue
State the prompt arrival of the all girl paramedic crew
Who at once, with calm and question, get to grips
And stabilise life with tourniquet and saline drips.
Then a voice is heard from the broken 'robin' shell,
"These two girls have earned their money well."

## How's a Bloke to Cope ?

Half the world are women, Lord,
And women a man can't afford.
So, how's a bloke to cope?
Which words are those that he should say
And which words are those, dear Lord,
That are much better left unspoken?

Women seem designed to mystify.
They mystify the likes of me.
So, how's a bloke to cope?
When am I supposed to stop and play
And this I ask, dear Lord,
When is it best to stay away?

How can we blokes tell, oh Lord,
When all is well and we have scored?
So, how's a bloke to cope;
Which signs are go, for they are green
And which are all those others, dear Lord,
You know - the ones they never mean?

When will I find peace with her, oh Lord?
For now is the time that I must know.
So, how's a bloke to cope?
What do I do when my bones decline?
Do I ask her to comfort me, dear Lord,
Until I'm in sight of my finishing line?

Look here, my son, when your days are done
You'll find up here they're just the same.
I, too, am a bloke who cannot cope,
So treasure your life and cherish it dear.
If you think, my son, that it's bad down there
You'll find it's far worse once you come up here.

## In Pursuit of Killing

Four men. Each different
Yet in essence just the same,
Set out with border collie, Spike,
And a mongrel with no name.
All, as keen of purpose,
Hid in November's falling gloom:
The carpenter, his mate,
The drayman, and dumb groom.

Bound in masks and shadows
For their harsh pursuit of game,
And in its execution
Brought down eternal shame;
Down upon the sawyer,
And his callow boy, of course,
The beer delivery man,
And mute keeper of the horse.

Among the unseen elms,
And misty, choking brier
They did fill a hiding keeper
With lead blasted shotgun fire;
To rip his wax-clothed skin
And cause a stomach churning spill
Of warm, digesting bowels
And bring about a horrifying kill.

A madness of common disbelief,
At a stroke, united them,
Choking on a gasp of knowledge
They could not again be honest men:
The God-forsaken joiner,
The crying boy gone mad,
The carter, now of bloody barrels,
And the silent stable lad.

Four men. Each different -
Yet in killing just the same;
Out with their keen hunting dogs,
Brought down poor human game.
None of them was caught
But trapped in life long gloom:
The carpenter, his mate,
The drayman, and dumb groom.

## Lambing

Ever diligent, the spare shepherd strides
On his march through April's early fog,
His urgent gait, stark in contrast
To his bounding, keen-eyed, working dog.
His boots, tight-laced and dubbined-brown,
Crush sods of frost-stiff-cobbled ground
In their earnest dash
To start the new season's lambing round.

At the old barn door he moves the prop
That serves to guard as bolt and lock.
Then, he leads the first rounded wave inside
To birth the bursting mother flock
Held in small corral of straw and hurdle pens,
Stood beneath a torched and tile roof
While the drying, earthen floor
Becomes compressed by boot and cloven hoof.

A new mother hears the tiny bleat
Of first twin, followed by a second cry,
As the standing flock of still full ewes,
In their expectant nervousness, stand by
Under sheltered patch of willow thatch,
Stiff legged and bound in broadened girth.
With horn-hard lips they tear sparse root
From the long-ill-giving limestone earth.

Discontent is aired from a border ewe
Until, she, in her turn, can spill from within
Her bloody, crying, eight-month load
And swell with tenor chords the bleating din.
Her nose nudging, cleaning, mothering,
She draws her twins to stand on all eight feet
And guides their unrelenting bleats
To find good sup from each tender, spilling teat.

New mothers fill the barn, discharging
Lambs quick in rising on unsteady feet,
While the shepherd takes his breath
Outside in rain fast turned to driving sleet.
An old green bottle filled with cold brown tea
Is necked to soak his balk of bread and cheese
Taken, sat on moss covered combers,
Beneath the bursting sticky buds of ageing conker trees.

Then he is back at the ovine quarry face
Under oil lamps, trimmed and right of wick,
Lit to show the wheezing evening jewels
Where to bite, and groom, and lick.
His clock-round shift has taken its toll,
Even his dancing dog no longer bounds
As they, on weary legs, shamble slowly home
Kept company by a flying screech of sounds.

His thoughts only on the bed
(That waits along the slick and ill-lit track)
Where, barefoot, he will gladly fall
To rest his weary limbs and stiffened back
Until – before the dawn can call -
He is out with dog, and crook, and striding reach
To birth those bleating mothers more
And bring his order to the lambing breach.

## The Living Tree

Green stick forced to bend -
split and scarred
where forced to mend,
and must ascend
for the light
to grow to journey's end.

Large trunk standing stout -
heavy limbs
cloaked when buds burst out.
Her blossoms shout,
" We're the best!"
Without recourse to doubt.

Spreading branch is nature's rest
beneath a canopy
to cowl a young bird's nest.
Confidence expressed
when brightly lit,
until darkly exit in the west.

Green are those that bear full leaf
in which
no fledge will come to grief.
Cocks sound relief
by whistling
gleeful songs of loud belief.

Blossom set turns to autumn fruit,
whetting palates'
hunger in fur and feather suit
which, though mute,
can live
through winters cold salute.

## A Love of Trout

If you are caught by love, you must not show
That your breast beats at a frantic pace
To a tune you do not, in essence, know,
Upon a drumhead, with a painted face,
By sticks extended; to leave you undefended
From finger's knife, honed to draw a naked sketch
In blood from a heart struck, but still unbended,
By sharp disquiet set to mortify a wounded wretch.

Think only of the coarse brown trout whose eye
Is turned to face the rapid, down-stream water flow
To feed, first on the dragon, then upon your dancing fly.
Lured and hooked, then held by a mighty casting blow
To dance a frantic jig upon your lissom spinning reel
Before his end comes as an entrée to your evening meal.

## Melting Ice and Liquid Snow

Still they could not cross the mighty river flow
For her banks they had spread to an awesome width
Swelled by tides of melting ice and liquid snow.

Paddle boats set out to cut the swell, and mow
With larger heads of steam and revolutions, but
Still they could not cross the mighty river flow.

Men sat at bow and stern in pairs to power row
Their timber craft, but could not span the reach
Swelled by tides of melting ice and snow.

They sat to wait till storm would drop her blow,
But she did not, and left sore knowledge that
Still they could not cross the mighty river flow.

They must seek the ferry chain a dozen feet below
In hope to pull their way across the open flood,
Swelled by tides of melting ice and liquid snow.

It was their last gasp drawn to cross the Ohio.
They pulled so hard that some were lost. But
Still they could not cross the mighty river flow,
Swelled by the tides of melting ice and snow.

## Mental Flight

Walking in the dark
is no fun for anyone
while all their friends
walk over in the sun.
It seems my life
is not writ to please
for I am seen as stale bread
with not even dried out cheese

I see the spider look
from his web to frown
at the common sparrow
flying upside down.
Both look down on me
but I'm no longer here
for the hopping frog
has made me disappear.

I arrange to take a friend
high up in the sky
where hurt and pain,
I know, just cannot fly.
So, I say a silent prayer
to help us quickly find
those pieces in the air
that once made up my mind.

Soaring high above
a pets' home in a cloud
I see a three-eared dog
reading 'War and Peace' aloud.
I come across a horse's head,
partnered with a pig,
practising their Scottish reels
by dancing an Irish jig.

So, my search grows frantic
now my friend has gone.
I talk to squirrels' holes in trees
who answer me as one,
" You must settle down below
and leave your hopes behind,
for those pieces left us long ago
that once made up your mind."

## Minding

Are my tears those of joy
Or are they those of pain?
I cannot tell my tears apart
As dew drop from fallen rain.
I feel the ghouls removing
Many of my body parts
Put, bloodstained, in plastic bags
And left where isolation starts.

I'm held in here by patients,
Used as iron bars,
Turning keys, to ordered words
Of doctors here from Mars.
Poison seeps around their lips
From fangs of venom teeth
Sunk deep into my fading wits
With no halt or pain relief.

Attempts are made to empty,
As I am in trance confined,
The confusion they see filed
Deep inside my tortured mind.
A mind beset with chemicals
Where silent demons cannot sleep,
For fear of drowning slowly
In the falls where rivers meet.

Family and friends come in
Who, in reality, are my foes
Carrying weapons done as gifts,
Wrapped, hidden in their clothes.
All the shrieking and the laughter
Hides their darkness from the light,
Driven on by motivations that
Are blacker than the night.

They strap me down for safety
As they probe my odd emotions,
Urged on by budget targets,
Backed up by pills and potions.
But I resist their created fear
And absorb the numbing pain,
For I am, amongst those held in here,
The only one completely sane.

## Nesting Sparrows

How hard the nesting sparrows work
as they dash, amid
their own incessant chatter,
in ever frantic rush,
to complete a nursery
fashioned, from soft discards,
under rooftop eaves
made of more substantial matter.

How bright the sparrows make the day
as they give voice
to songs, composed inside their heads,
flitting in annoyance
among the gathering starlings,
for furnishings dropped
by those speckled interlopers
and taken under eaves
to complete fresh feather beds.

How earnestly the sparrows push
their fine ounces,
in ever demanding sinuous strife,
exhorting each effort
of their endless comings and goings,
for April's completion date
of nursery under the eaves
where they start upon their family life.

How warm the morning's dawn
with sweet chorus
sung between the hours of four and five,
followed by a breakfast
of midges taken high upon the wing
and scraps of carrion
won in battles raged with finches
and taken under eaves
in a desperate need for food to survive.

How proudly the nesting sparrows chirp
as they announce,
in more incessant chatter,
the ever frantic rush
to feed a greedy brood,
with part digested soft discards,
under rooftop eaves -
now become a growing family matter.

## Never Having Been

Shadows break unseen,
Through clouds of misshapen forms,
Lost in colourless distraction
Before the unfulfilling dawn
Drawn by the chill
Of ice flows
To be frozen in a constant state.
*The state of never having been*

Shadows rent unseen,
By harsh tares, to splash
On the wind-whipped stream,
Boiling to all the compass points,
Light and shade driven,
To mix and then scatter
As no more than floating ashes.
*The ashes of never having been*

Shadows, trapped unseen,
Of demons breathing,
With their rasping bark of shivers,
To soak in freezing sweat
The tightly bound nude torso
Shackled to the sleeper's
Contorted, wretched, distant nightmare.
*The nightmare of never having been*

Shadows, cast unseen
By soulless, sprawling monoliths,
Block out creation's wish
To shape, and flow, and form with nature;
To stifle free will's trial
Set to contend blind obedience
And vanquish mortal suffocation.
*The suffocation of never having been*

Shadows fall unseen
Upon the wizen, fruitless trees.
They fall from long-forgotten dreams
Cast by long-forgotten beings
Unseen in after-life
As they once were
When alive, in constant dread.
*The dread of never having been*

## Overcast Dismay

Invading wet attacks the trees
To hold them in a veil of mist,
Have them fade,
Blur their right to light,
Enshroud their leafy greeting,
And reduce the blackbird's song to bleating.

It grounds the flying bumble bees
And soaks leg-hairs that do not stand
About the nectar flutes
To take a honey-weight and by doing pollinate
Each stamen shoot
To ensure a summer rich in fruit.

Saturating wet blows squall and breeze
To drown the strands of frail nest,
Spread in disarray,
And cause the busy hen to start again
In earnest on her work so late,
She only squawks to chide her livid mate.

It brings pallid lilies to their knees,
Blows dropped white petals
Like scattered, dampened linen
As though spread by thieves of silken handkerchiefs
Sold for immoral gain
And notoriety brought about by lack of shame.

Hailstones batter as they please
Horse chestnut and lilac candles
And tip tulip begging bowls,
Desperate for feed to pollinate their seed,
Now hooded, bowed, and bent
Like starving monks towards the end of Lent.

Constant damp brings old men to wheeze,
Through whiskers, bristling
Grey about their gargled throats,
Cleared of dust and phlegm,
And to say, without a doubt,
"Ner cast a clout afore the end of May is out."

## Plantation House

Cockroaches long had left Her
To mould and dry rot spores
That flourished in the rafters
And down beneath the floors.
Rot had aged Her carcass
Brought to a wretched plight
And Her livery, long since chipped,
Presents a sore dilapidated sight.

Will youngsters ever dance
Once again upon Her porch
Where I once danced the night,
Lit by fire and flaming torch?
Reels and jigs to fiddles,
A two-step to fife and drum
Attempt the Dashing Sergeants,
As the soldiers yet to come.

Will Her redwood lounge
Once again in joy resound
To those intoxicating bars
Of a past Glen Miller sound?
Or hear chinking crystal glasses,
At the drinking of the toasts,
By happy, bright young voices
Giving thanks to their good hosts?

Will we see again prepared
Upon Her wood fire stove
The giblets of a critter
Caught in the mango grove?
Or a meal baked in sunflower oil;
Fillets of fresh caught fish,
Bathed in a white wine sauce,
Served from a silver dish?

Will Her creaking bedroom floors
Ever feel the pacing feet
Of a nervous, sweating father,
Waiting for the chance to greet
His new born, crying child
For whom his straining wife,
Through her exhausting labours,
Has brought the right to life?

I fear for Her near future
In the turmoil of this place,
For She stands a symbol of
The old supremacy of race.
Will pleas for preservation pass
Right through her open hall,
Unheard among the ghastly thump
Of the demolition ball?

# The Ploughman

Behind the ledged and braced back door,
Once bright but darker now,
Lives a man whose life was spent
A-following of the horse and plough.
Breaking sleep to step at dawn,
He walked many a mile to lunch,
Behind the wooden handled shafts
And lumbering Suffolk Punch.

The single furrow lone and long
Is trod, by measured gait of feet,
Laced in splitting hobnail boots,
Behind the pulling Trojan's seat.
To headland turns the rounding blade
Through clay and stony loam,
Then back they step in harmony
Along the furrow leading home.

The acres ploughed are black,
Shimmering silver by noon light,
Giving up those worms and grubs
To flocking crows demanding bite.
The squawking of the carrion
Calls the starlings to their prey
Of regal scraps that fall
Until darkness takes the day.

At certain times the seasons rise,
Or in fading light they fall,
Baked by summer's scorching heat,
Or withered by inclement squall.
Through these extremes
The ploughman never leaves his course,
As, with coat tails flat or dancing,
He stays behind his plodding horse.

Years break down the ground;
Wear out the man and horse.
The Punch is boxed and canned
And the ploughman's spent of force.
Different shires now draw the plough
While youngsters follow on behind.
Past deeds and men - forgotten -
Gone from the earth and mind.

## Rachel

The joy of Rachel
Is the wisdom of one
So good, gifted, and bright.
Her heart closed her life
But her wisdom remains,
Caught in our deeds
And held in our thoughts.
They are free of dark night
Who walk in her light,
Cheered by her grace
And warmed by
Her fairness of face.

## Rachel, Farewell.

Organ music cannot quell
The falling tears
Of mourners dressed
In their sombre best.

A notice saying:
By request: No flowers,
Now in streaks
From rain of several hours.

Umbrellas up
To top the hush
Of those few
Grieving at the grave.

The sad remains
Of one, once so bright,
Are lowered -
Slowly out of sight.

Mourners leaving.
Family bowed and grieving.
A mother - without life -
Now eternal spirit-wife.

## Raging Night

Blackness overtakes the light
As darkness falls
And quiet emptiness arrives
To fill the void
With daytime bustle gone from sight,.
But now, strangely bright,
As fire consumes the dark
To paint the sky
As an over orange night.

So stillness now is brushed aside,
Startled into consciousness
As men set off
From the resting station
On their frantic engine ride.
Not awake enough
To dress with thought just yet,
But still arriving, gas tight,
With ladder, hose, and pride.

The bowed roof disgorges haphazard, barking fire.
Yellow haloes, misshaped
Like grotesque ghosts,
Are pulled from sleep to dance
Like marionettes, hung from their performing wire,
Each angered that they had
To wear an orange coat,
And cloud of crowning purple gas
Put on to feed the blazing pyre.

Pink and mandarin flame
Are engaged in free-style wrestling
On their unsure release.
Arms and legs in fractious tangle,
Each desperate for an hour of fame,
Before the fighters put them out
So they can then investigate,
Find the careless culprits,
And to them apportion blame.

Flame now leaves to smoke
The distortion of the night
With her uncoloured pall of suffocation,
Cruelly taking air from lungs
Causing men to choke,
Hanging over all,
Like Satan's wicked veil,
To sting the sightless streaming eyes
And burst their lungs beneath His cloak.

A blast of wind. And red sparks spout
In a spiral, spitting upwards,
In desperate need to threaten those too close
Before they tumble earthwards
And their glow is lost to doubt.
While the soaking hose lays claim
To the char and ash,
With the spreading water blanket
That sees the fire's gasping breath give out.

## Reality

I'm not the man I want to be.
I am the man life made of me.
First my mind and body whole,
Then my mortal heart and soul,
Taken by men for reformation;
To fit into their dream of nation.
A child processed; once again
Cast in concrete, steel, and chain.

The man I am I have been made.
It's not the part I should have played.
I run from artisan and metal man,
Designed and built in Birmingham.
While fleeing from the factory gate
I strip off the wires and armour plate.
Now, disconnected, I'm undetected,
Home - free, clean, and uninfected.

Life and times will take away
The breath I need so I can play
The music of the Celtic Isles,
Creating Gaelic lasses' smiles,
Eating love's forbidden berries
Aboard the ancient sailing ferries,
Drifting over the endless tide
Of breakers formed on ocean side.

I reach for the height of aspiration
Now released from dank incarceration.
The free ideas, fresh in thought,
Are my own - not something bought.
I live to some in sore disgrace,
Not a part of *their* human race.
But I am the man I want to be -
Not the man they made of me.

## Remembrance

I've heard the awful cries
Of men injured in this war
And now hope that one day I
Will chance to hear
Them singing, free of pain.
But in truth, my boy,
I know that they are drowned,
Sucked under mud and rain.

I've seen many good men go;
Cut by steel, blown apart,
Or frozen in the snow.
Perhaps not lost
But rescued before too long.
But in truth, my boy,
I hear the chaplain's words
And know that they have gone.

I've spent long nights
Waiting for the battle charge
In the hope that each day
I will chance to be
Among the soldiers who survive.
But in truth, my boy,
I feel that time will not
Send me back home alive.

I've walked the length
Of many a well worn track
In the hope one day I
Will chance upon
The home where I belong.
But in truth, my boy,
I have to say
I've lingered here too long.

I've seen the bugler
Drawn to his full height
And hoped to hear him play
But my ears are deaf
To my own Last Post
For I'm in the past, my boy,
As death has taken my body
And the Devil has my ghost.

## Rhubarb

We'd goo t'Paxford rabbitin'
Where we'd meet wi' ol' Frank Payne.
Ol' Frank 'e wuz a wise man who
Explained t'me the need fer wind an' rain.
It wuz t'make the crops grow
On the land 'e worked fer Farmer Stokes
What grew the vegetable Trinity
So they called 'im the 'oly Ghost.

I asked 'im to explain this Trinity
So I could understand.
Frank said, "We only needs three veg fer 'ealth
An' we grows 'em on this land.
We grows the spuds to give
Folks the strength t' get about.
The sprouts are grown t'loosen you
An' the rhubarb t' clear you out."

Farmer Stokes grew rhubarb
In the fields an' forcin' sheds.
'e employed some travellin' workers
What slept in barrack beds.
They put some o' the crop in bottles
An' some more in gret big tins.
Ol' Frank told me, " If she ate enough
Your wife, she would 'ave twins."

Then 'e asked me if I wuz clear
Why it wuz important t'control
All animals what damage the crops
Like the rabbit, mouse, an' mole.
I just nodded back to 'im
Finding it a lot to be takin' in.
Rememberin' that 'e told me once
Rhubarb could cure a double chin.

Everybody done best they could
But, though we all worked very 'ard,
We couldn't stop the rumours
An' gloom set in around the yard.
'Cos the times they wuz a-changin'
The fruit game 'ad took a tumble
And as the Journal 'eadline sadly read,
"PAXFORD FOLK SEE THEIR RHUBARB CRUMBLE."

## Seniors' Service

Who are we - sad, cast out
To an ordered life of ease,
Described as 'Oh, those seniors
Or simply O.A.Ps'?
Pensioners, without a voice,
Silenced by impoverishment
And our senility as perceived
By a pompous Government.

We learned to read and write
In town and village schools;
To work for King and Country
And never break the rules.
We formed a good defence
And, on calling, went to war
To fight for dear Motherland
And risk death upon foreign shore.

We laid the iron tracks
And drove the speeding trains,
Conquered the art of flight
And flew the aeroplanes,
Built many caring hospitals
With concrete, steel and brick,
Trained to be the doctors
Who worked to cure the sick.

We built the roads and bridges
Over mountain, glen, and fall,
Motorised the horse and cart
To bring benefits to us all,
Tended to the stock and crops
In meadow, lea, and field,
Using years of knowledge gained
For an ever improving yield.

We paid our rates and taxes
And backed the Bevan scheme
To build a caring nation
In the Labour post-war dream.
With the Tories we paid the same
To raise a younger generation
Who would then, in their turn,
Look after our proud nation.

We're told there was not near enough
Paid into the pension pot -
So a Health Department spokesman says,
"That's it. You've had your lot!
We can't afford the treatment
To reward your selfless dedication -
So we must make you pay again
And seek private medication."

Now our limbs are stiff
And we need a little care.
We're informed by answer phone
There's simply no one there.
Appointments, made for weeks to come,
Leave us with this simple dread :
Who will we be meeting first –
The doctor or the dead?

## The Soldier Ash

A line of ashes on Kingcombe Lane
For years have made their stand,
Like British soldiers sent to fight
In some far flung, foreign land.
Dressed in khaki coloured leaves
They stare towards the dawn of day
From where attacking clouds may come
Dressed in black and field grey.

So long have the soldier ashes stood,
Determined never to give ground.
Their bodies bear the battle scars
Caught in defence of their surround.
Some bent, some bowed, some down,
And some show signs of amputation -
All scarred and gnarled and blackened
By all those years of conflagration.

An old woman walks towards me,
My thoughts on trees once more,
So, I am surprised to hear her tell
Of the men she's lost through war;
Her father died on the field of Ypres,
Her uncle gone, on the banks of the Somme,
Her brother and lover fell in the east,
And now they will never come home.

The old woman lets out a cry
As she hears the marching boots
Of a forest of khaki troops
Grown over black and ashen roots.
Then the crack of a grave attack
Brings crashing down an ash
Brought, split, to the ground
By the bolt of a lightning flash.

Clouds of ash leaves fall from the tree
Like men from a Pals' Brigade
Charging in force; set on a course
Of attack with bullet and blade.
Each seed that falls to the ground
Marks the soul of a soldier
Sent to the warmth of the spirits;
No more to suffer from cold here.

## South Flows the Burn

From the birthing, craggy darkness
Of a mountain's cavern chill,
Bursts a new arrival
For her introduction to the sight
Of homely hills set in a sunlit splash.
She has no time to chat
As she must dash.
With relish and with force
Her energy, in crystal clarity, runs,
And tumbles, in babblings
Only good Nature will understand,
To fall by gravity's unspoken command.

Sightless, brakeless, churning speeds
Take her onwards
To the waiting, silent brine,
To be sore adulterated
By salt, and sea, and time.
She gasps, unheard by swimmers
In their own life race;
Caught up in swift survival's pace -
Floating, diving, travelling south
Small devoured by each larger mouth,
As Nature in her ocean swell unheard
Will still dictate the final word.

She exists, not in mortal form
And is gone from all but weather's sight,
Now in a sudden flash
By solar rays into freshness saved
From brine inflicted wave
To be well-suited in her vapour stage.
Now, re-formed in purity,
She rains down on mountain range
That once was, and shall again,
Become her birthing house
When droplets, running filtered pure,
Start their journey south once more.

## Spring Music

The bowed white bells of praying winter drops
Will, in time, give way to yellow flower and orange tops
Of Easter trumpets stood upon their hard green stilts
Until withdrawn to brown as each one wilts,
Then leaves the apple blossom's pink and white array
To burst about their orchard home in spring display
That draws the bee to call, while he is passing by,
And holds the muse's wonder through a soulful eye.

O daffodils, you brought calm to March Lion's roar.
You are the sign that shows the end of winter's dark once more;
The beacon to light the long awaited bright new spring,
Your bells resound as loud as those that any churches ring.
I salute your challenge to the winter buccaneer
And hold you to return to march each year on year.

## Springs Past

Winter's frosty grip must give
For new life to start to live.
As rushing streams ever faster flow,
And on their racing journeys go.
Waters now have quickened speed
Through meadows filled with waking seed,
While stirring mice and cousin voles
Sniff spring's air from wintering holes.

I look with some surprise
Through the windows of my eyes
To see that spring is strewn
From mid-March on into June.
March brings winds for flying kites
Over the top of man-made sights -
Like broken sails on deserted mills,
Ringed with yellow daffodils.

Nature takes this time to change
Develop, gallop, and rearrange
Dormant bulbs and bursting buds,
Mad March hares in conker woods,
Preening cocks that do their best
To build a homely, well-lined nest
In oak, and ash, and willow wood
For their feathered parenthood.

Hawthorn bud when hawthorn's green,
Most vivid green as can be seen.
Hanging catkins – yellow, new –
Framed in webs soaked by clear dew.
Hints of green upon the trees
Is nature's invitation to the bees,
Written in dappled pink and white
Blossom, lit by morning light.

The high blue sky's a gripping sight,
Leaking storm clouds in greys and white,
Sending warmth and April showers
Ordered on by nature's powers,
Starting below in worm turned loam
To produce a bulging 'Harvest Home.'
Fortunate am I such spring attraction
Brings me such a dear distraction.

## The Stone Dressing

I hear the high pitched chatter
Of bludgeon axes falling
To dress the undressed stone,
Bringing flakes, like walnut fists
Or flat as autumn leaves,
Falling round the banker's block
As if to mock
The dusted chocolate loam.

The wind picks up the frosty chill
And sets about
To blow the unblown canvas sheeting
Which serves as bankers' threadbare roof
And head wear for the stone,
Lying in drops of blasted, waiting,
Near anticipating
The mason's percussion-hammer greeting.

I hear the treble tone of ringing
As the chiming axes fall
To square the unsquared stone
In high-pitched timpani,
As clappers find their tuning marks,
Then fill the frost clear air
And banker's hair
With dust he cannot comb.

Cloud billows from the punctured drum,
Brought in with picks
To fume the bivouac with non-perfume of coke,
Stinging bloodshot eyes already reddened
By the flying limestone scree,
As airborne shrapnel smithereens surprise
Those salty eyes
Now half blinded by the angry smoke.

But copper-banded, ruddy wrists do not stop
But rain the axes down
In battle sounds, resounding to the marrow bone,
Without respite from cold and pain.
They cleave to shape and tail,
Those ragged balls of rugged lime
Into the fine,
Advancing piles of finished building stone.

## The Thrashing Drum

I remember well the thrashing drum,
Admired by many, cursed by some.
Such a mighty harvesting machine
Its likes to us had never been seen.
Metal made with metal parts,
Standing next to wooden carts.
Leather belts with endless seam
Joined to tractor, powered by steam.

First we made the tractor boil
Ready for the hard day's toil.
Water in the tank we'd pour,
Coal in through the fire box door.
Crackling sparks spitting rage
Is how the drum would earn a wage.
So much energy it would seem
Generated by compressing steam.

Work began with instant dust
From the dried and empty husk.
Tractor smoke hanging in the air
And rats a running everywhere.
Then with sinews taut we'd heave
Up to the drum those barley sheaves.
It was even harder on our backs
When carrying away the corn filled sacks.

Hour after hour we'd have to smell
Heated grease and oil, as well
As smoking embers invading the nose
And hanging forever in our clothes.
Our guts did make an empty rattle
Glad of food they fed to cattle.
Then a few minutes for us to please
Our bellies with dry bread and cheese.

The farmer demands much less talk
And much more movement from the fork.
I know just where I'd like to stick
Both the prongs of my old shuppick.
But I toss those sheaves and then some
On to the top of that thrashing drum.
Another rat runs across my toe
But I'm so tired I let him go.

Eating, breathing, coughing empty husk,
I'm slowly filled from dawn to dusk.
If, while on the drum I stride
And slip through the top to fall inside,
They'd find, if I was cut in half,
I'm just a bag filled up with chaff,
Discoloured by the smoke and ember
Tanned from dawn until September.

Today, the air-conditioned combine
Does the work that once took nine.
The machine that turns out giant bales
Has replaced the sheaves and winnowing flails.
No more corn sacks on good men's backs
Or treading loft boards with shakes and cracks.
But most of all I see the end has come
For that well remembered thrashing drum.

## Uncle

*Is Uncle here?*
Well no, my dear,
He doesn't live here anymore.
He went off with the boys who lived next door.
They went late last night
To join the fight
Against the bloody Boer.
By now, my dear, they'll be marching off to war.

*Has Uncle returned?*
Yes, my dear, but badly burned.
He came home quite late last night,
Sick and tired of that awful fight,
With just one of the boys who live next door.
The other will stay abroad for evermore.
All that remains to remind his Mam
Of her young lad is the black-edged Army telegram.

*Is Uncle better?*
Yes, my dear. He's received the letter
To say he's fit
So he's returned to his job down the pit.
He's so delighted
That he's been invited,
After all this time,
To work back in that coal-rich mine.

*Is Uncle in?*
Yes, my dear. I wish you'd come and speak to him
Because the news once more
Is talk of 'the war to end all wars.'
Now off we stride,
He with me close by his side.
With bands and cheers and sentiment
We join the local regiment.

*Is Uncle shot?*
Yes. That's him, lying in a cot,
His legs left in a heap
On the battle field at Ypres.
Next day at one
His life was gone.
No man I knew more brave,
His legless, lead filled body now hidden in the grave.

*Are those Uncle's affairs?*
Yes. These are the sum of his worldly wares.
All that is left of him,
Wrapped in a parcel tied with string :
His snuff box and pocket knife
Remind me of a greatly shortened life;
A package, sent by second post,
With no joy for the son now turned to ghost.

*Is Uncle there?*
Yes. But you must prepare
To leave and yield
Your body to the Flander's field.
You were both so badly led
Into death. Your bodies bled.
Your lost souls, so pure,
Will be man's burden evermore.

## The Waiting Room

Through the waltzing doors
They come, in dribs and drabs,
Dropped off by bus, or car,
Or out of taxi cabs.
They walk across the floor
To such a shoe led clatter
It sounds as though their feet
Are here only for the natter.

Mothers, with young children
Strapped in their buggy prams,
Advance, panzer like,
As formation battering rams.
With appointments tightly held,
They queue with not an utter
Until they're asked their names
And then they hardly mutter.

"Please take a seat and wait......
Yes, anyone. You choose,"
Are the sister's kindly words.
She speaks softly to soothe.
She says we're right on time.
But disbelief is in our eyes
As she's obliged, once more, to tell
The same old pack of lies.

The clock goes on its rounds,
As the caring doctors should,
But still there are no specialists
To stem the patient flood.
More and more unwell appear
Through the dancing doors,
To occupy the cushioned seats
And sit upon the polished floors.

Then there is a call for
A certain Mrs Evelyn Endright.
Who is here for laser treatment
To improve her failing sight.
She is a lady who, when walking,
Has a tendency to wobble,
And is supported by a greying man
Who, at best, can only hobble.

But the doctors are unseen,
In their clean white coats.
We're told they will be ready
When they've read the patients' notes.
No one else is called,
As the staff group in a huddle,
In an attempt to find a way
Of sorting out the awful muddle.

A porter leans against a wall,
While a nurse is heard to say,
"Yesterday, I thought was bad
but it's even worse today."
Triumphant women volunteers
Bring cakes and start to pour
Some rather greyish tea that could
Be left over from the War.

A little girl is sick
While her baby sister cries.
A lady's questions get nowhere
But at least she tries.
A man with plastered wrist
Can't seem to find the loo
As most folk sit and vegetate
With nothing else to do.

A call for Mrs Black
Followed by one for Mr Banks
Means that I am next –
A cause for giving thanks.
Dr Goodday calls me in
And asks if I am well.
Before I finish my reply,
He says, "Next," and rings the bell.

The nurse says, "The doctor's pleased
With the way you have progressed
But now you seem all on edge.
Are you a bit depressed?"
Then I'm given counselling
And when asked to please explain
I reply, "It's just the thought
Of having to come back here again."

## White Roads

Snow falls, in her own quiet wanderings,
To bring disorder to the leaving day
And comes to rest
On quickly over-coated roads
And roofs, of tile and slate,
Forced, without recourse, to bear her unwelcome weight.

Snow, by wheels compressed from crystals
Into glistening, highly polished ice,
Takes away
The treaded tyre's grip
To cause a self inflicted long delay
Upon the homeward, ice-bound, chill highway.

Snow's myriad of glittering, virgin flakes
Come to ground, like tongueless skeins
Of landing geese,
Escaping from the arctic
To settle south, as the lightest fall of snow
With which to slow the urgent traffic flow.

Snow's white hue is turned to sad, electric pink
With the lighting of street neon lamps.
And pale moon's
Pastel yellow loses out
To this source of man-made light
Where she, alone, once lit the darkened night.

Snow, by wheels mixed into a brown repulse
Now frozen into dark night's vice,
Traps the traveller
In abandoned conveyance
Or forces him to slip, and slide
With angry words and spilling pride.

Snow falls, as she does in her sudden winter ways,
To catch us all in an old surprise;
With snow clearing
Lost in a planning haze.
Then, by her nature does succumb
And leaves us rescued by the warming of a welcome sun.

Snow has now removed to her hiding place,
To wait and watch, preparing for
Her next
Bombing blitz attack;
To send us into in shelter's hell
Away from yet more snow that without permission fell.

## Yuletide Yesterday

You tells me there's nothin' can be done
T' save my wife and starvin' son
But you be lit by fire and candle light
T' warm you on the coldest night
With fresh picked vegetables there to eat,
Sat on plates of tasty roasted meat.
Yon lurcher be a-gnawin' on a bone
Finer than any victuals in my 'ome.

You leaves me stood out in the yard
Tellin' me just 'ow 'hard
Your family's suffered here of late,
Starin' at an empty grate.
But bisn't they an' bisn't thee
A-sittin' round the Christmas tree,
Singin' songs of stars an' gold
While I be 'ere stood in the cold?

"To you, master, I do implore!"
But with that 'e do close the door
On my word an' in my face,
As though I'm just an empty space.
With now no reason for to stay
I slowly turns an' walks away,
Drawn along the cobbled street
Echoin' t'my 'obnailed feet.

I cannot return with empty 'and.
I 'ave t' borrow from off the land.
Through the alder 'edge I push,
Ripped by thorns on brier bush.
I feel the blood runnin' thin
An' flowin' warm across my skin.
I lift my arm an' quickly lick
With 'unger pains an' feelin' sick.

Pullin' taters from a berry -
Not enough for makin' merry.
Just enough, I lift the latch,
An' offer them to my starvin' batch.
Then off into the dead of night
Under darkness takin' flight.
Back to empty plate an' spoon
Seen only by the freezin' moon.

I catch my toe an' fall right there
Onto a rabbit caught in a snare.
From that wire I sets 'is spirits free
An' take his body back 'ome for tea.
I shows my family what I've brought
Taters an' rabbit, freshly caught.
We thanks the Lord on Christmas Day
An' prays for poverty t' go away.